MW00890580

Cover and book design, illustrations © 2009 Bentley Holmes-Gull. For additonal information about the artist, visit www.bentleyhg.com.

Copyright © 2009
ISBN 1442117710

All rights reserved. No part of this book may be reproduced in any format or any medium without the written permission of the author.

For additonal information about the author, visit www.childrensimaginings.com.

This book is dedicated to the children of Zambia,
with love.

Imagine That...
A Picture Book of Possibilities

by
Rosemary Holmes - Gull

Illustrated by
Bentley Holmes - Gull

There are so many people in this big wonderful world of ours...

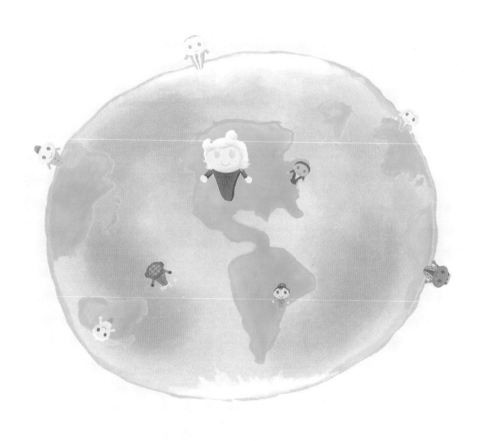

Do you sometimes feel lost and confused?

Look around you, there are wonders in nature that can help you to understand your own magnificence.

Just look around at our incredible world. See if you can find the lessons...

Take a look at the tiny ant.
Did you ever think an ant could teach you something?

Even though an ant is small, it can carry up to 50 times its own weight...pretty impressive, huh!

That would be like us lifting a car.

Imagine that...

Imagine that you have great power like the ant.

You **are** important.

When you discover your power, just imagine what you can become.

First you have to believe, and then you'll find the way to achieve.

Are you discouraged when bad things happen to you?

Perhaps you have lost someone special in your life, or you've been disappointed by a friend.

Is life sometimes a struggle for you?

Let's look at something else in nature...the butterfly.

Have you ever watched the tiny butterfly struggling to get free of the chrysallis? It's very hard work for that tiny pupa to wriggle free, but did you know that the effort to get out of that tiny opening in the chrysallis is very necessary? It forces fluids from the swollen body into the wings, so they will be strong enough to fly.

Imagine that...

Imagine that when things get really difficult for you, it's actually an opportunity to grow.

You can do it!

When you face challenges...all you have to do is believe you are bigger than your struggles, and then you'll find a way to grow.

Do you sometimes feel that learning something new is impossible?

Like tying your shoelaces, for example.

It's so much easier to get someone else to do it for you, and it sure is quicker, isn't it?

But you have to learn to believe in the magnificence of you!

Think of a bumblebee. Did you know that his body is too big to fly on his tiny wings?

By all the rules of math and science, it is an impossibility.

Since no one told the bumblebee that, he just goes ahead and does it anyway.

While he's busy gathering nectar to make honey, he moves pollen from one plant to another. This is called pollination and without it many fruits and flowers would not grow.

Next time you bite into a juicy apple or smell a beautiful flower, remember the bee, the one who isn't supposed to fly.

Imagine that...

Imagine what great things you will add to the world when you do **your** impossible.

First you have to believe, then you'll find the way to achieve.

Look in the mirror—what do you see?
Do you see how amazing you are?

Of everything in this beautiful world - the animals, insects, flowers, and trees...

You are the best and finest creation because you have your imagination.

Your imagination can tell you wonderful things:

It whispers that you **are** strong. You **can** achieve your dreams.

It reminds you that you are tough enough to get through your struggles.

And reassures you that yes, **you can do the impossible!**

Imagine that...

About the Author

Rosemary Holmes-Gull

Rosemary Holmes-Gull B.Sc., M. Ed., was in elementary education for 30 years, first as a teacher of young children and later in teacher education. Now in her retirement she is following her passion to inspire and motivate through her writing.

For more information, and Rosemary's Blog, please visit:
www.childrensimaginings.com

About the Illustrator

Bentley Holmes-Gull

Bentley Holmes-Gull graduated from the Art Institute of Las Vegas with a BS in Video Game Art and Design. Bentley hopes to create interactive games for children that promote education and cooperation.

He is currently working as a freelance artist and game designer.

To learn more about the illustrator, visit:
www.bentleyhg.com

Mothers
Without Borders

www.motherswithoutborders.org

Our Vision

We envision a world where children are safe and loved,
understand their value, and are given opportunities to
thrive, grow, and contribute to their world in
meaningful ways.

We envision a world where children's voices are heard -
where caring adults join together to provide access to
clean water, nutritious food, safe
shelter, education, and medical care for all children,
especially those who are alone and without advocacy.

---

*The author is proud to be donating a portion of the
proceeds from this book to this wonderful
organization.*

14556725R00015

Made in the USA
Lexington, KY
05 April 2012